W9-CDS-429

Techniques to Improve Your Writing Skills

Revised and Expanded Edition

Written by Robert L. Iles
Edited by National Press Publications

NATIONAL PRESS PUBLICATIONS
6901 West 63rd Street • P.O. Box 2949 • Shawnee Mission, Kansas 66201-1349
1-800-258-7246 • 1-913-432-7757

Techniques to Improve Your Writing Skills
Published by National Press Publications
© 1989 National Press Publications

Printed in the United States of America

9 10

ISBN 1-55852-025-2

To Dave, for ideas. To Judy, for confidence.
To Phyl, for everything.

Table of Contents

INTRODUCTION

Bob Iles' *Techniques To Improve Your Writing Skills* is the *Boy Scout Handbook* of business writers. It tells you exactly what you need to survive in the *furor scribendi* wilderness. And what you don't need isn't in it.

Take this for example. Bob doesn't hit us over the head with every grammar rule ever written. He knows that would only clog our brains and keep our words from ever reaching paper. So what he does is tell us the only two rules we can't break under any circumstances.

Imagine! Only two rules to keep in mind. You won't have felt this free since you got your driver's license.

And that's not all. Bob knows the answers to all those questions about writing you always wanted to ask but know nobody could answer. Like the four things every memo should contain or the six myths about the people who read what you write or the fourteen word-pairs that seem to have been created just to affect (or is it effect?) the way we write.

The list goes on. And some of it may be familiar territory. We all know what that's like: *Sominex*. But not here. Bob keeps us going through even the driest material. Learning how to use quotation marks while reading about the client who spent a weekend in Atlantic City with his "wife," for instance, gives us all the intrigue of "Dynasty" without the gore. Or the commercials.

In fact, Bob is so sure you'll read his book *and* improve your writing, he's included a section on how to copyright your material. Now that's confidence!

Best feature of all? The book's length: 48 pages. Just right for people who don't have time to read.

Richard Andersen
James Thurber Writer-in-Residence
Ohio State University

WRITING—SKILL, NOT TALENT

"Writing is a skill, like golf. Some persons are naturally good at it, most are not, but all can improve with practice, especially if guided by proper instruction."

King, LS: *Why Not Say It Clearly, A Guide to Scientific Writing.*
Boston, Little, Brown and Co, 1978, p 19.

Unless you're aiming for the Nobel prize, you shouldn't be concerned about your writing talent. Writing good business documents is a craft, not an art. It requires skill, not talent, and you can learn skills.

You improve your writing skills the same way you improve your golf skills—practice and instruction. And you learn to write the way you learn to swim—you have to jump in and do it yourself. No amount of instruction will help if you don't get in and splash around.

A technique that has worked for many: write something every business day. Even if you don't let anyone else read it, write a little something. You'll get in the habit of judging it yourself, seeing where you might have written things better. With a little practice every day, you can get better at almost anything.

ONLY TWO
UNBREAKABLE RULES

If you examine the work of notable writers in any field, you'll find that all of them knowingly or unknowingly break many of the textbook rules of writing. William Faulkner, Thomas Wolfe, Kurt Vonnegut, Malcolm Forbes, Peter Drucker, Alan Abelson—all bend the language to their own uses.

But there are two rules that they and every other good writer follow: (1) know your subject, and (2) know your audience.

Know your subject. If you don't know something, you can't write it. The better you know something, the better—and easier—you will write.

Here's a good test to use on yourself before you write something: see if you can explain it *in your own words* to someone who knows less about it than you do. If so, you're ready to write. If not, you need to go back and do some more studying.

Know your audience. That's the other half of the basis of good writing. Before you begin to write, ask yourself such questions as:

- What do my readers *want* to know?
- What do they *need* to know?
- What are their *biases*, their *blind spots*?
- What *decisions* will be based on what I tell them?

If you're trying to *get agreement* on a proposal or a budget, you need to know your readers' current views on those matters.

If you're writing to *increase their knowledge*, you need to know how much they already know.

If you're trying to *change how they do something*, you may want to know why they use their present methods.

If you're trying to *get action*, you need to know what motivates them.

DON'T MAKE IT DIFFICULT: FOUR WAYS TO SIMPLIFY THE WRITING TASK

No first-draft masterpieces. A sculptor makes a few sketches of what he or she is going to sculpt, then makes a small clay model before doing the full-scale piece.

An engineer has the plan of the bridge set down on paper and in his or her head before he or she puts up the lasting steel.

When you are working on a long or complex piece of writing, you should do the same. Get a plan in front of you and do some drafting before you produce your final version.

One job at a time. Keep separate jobs separate. Don't proofread, look up correct spellings or worry about punctuation while you are drafting the first version. Just capture your thoughts on paper. When you have your thoughts on paper, then you can polish, correct and shorten your work.

Don't try to revise your writing when you or someone else is doing the final typing. That leads to endless numbers of "final" versions, and neither you nor your typist will do them with proper care because you both expect there will be another "final" version.

Drafting, revising, typing and proofreading are separate jobs that need their own kind of attention and their own time. Keep them separate.

Write for minutes, not hours. How long can you keep your concentration on a piece of business reading? Whatever that figure is, cut it in half to find out how long you can keep your concentration on your writing. If you can *read* business materials for half an hour before your concentration slips, you can probably *write* for about 15 minutes before you need a break.

Yes, you could write for two or three hours if you had to. But would your work at the end of the first hour be as good as your work in the first 20 minutes? What would it be like at the end of the second hour? And would you be happy about doing your next writing job if you slaved for three hours straight on your last one?

Most people write best if they take a break every 10—20 minutes. Others are most productive when they stay on a roll for five minutes, take a short break, then come back and write for another five minutes. Find your best pace and don't worry about looking busy every minute. When you are writing, *activity doesn't always equal productivity*. Some of your best writing comes from leaning back, staring at the ceiling, and thinking.

Be a good boss to yourself. Suppose your boss took you by the scruff of the neck, pointed to a chair and told you to sit down and write something by four o'clock and said, "And it better be perfect, too."

We do that to ourselves sometimes when there is a writing job to be done. Imagine how one of your employees would react to that treatment. Resentment, low motivation, reluctance to work unless watched over with a whip. That's the way *you* react to *yourself* when you don't have:

- reasonable deadlines, enough time to do a good job.
- a clear idea of the purpose, the good that is going to come out of the work.
- an understanding of how the job should be done.
- the right materials to work with (dictionary, source documents, the chance to talk to experts, a good place to write).
- expectation of a reward.

A GIANT STEP TO IMPROVEMENT: KNOW WHY, NOT JUST WHAT

There are two approaches to improving your writing. One is to look for faults and correct them, one by one. That's the Chinese-water-torture approach. You find mistake after mistake and there seems to be no end. In fact, there isn't, for there will always be mistakes in writing. You'll find them even in Shakespeare's work.

Another approach offers the possibility of big improvements soon.

Know *why* you're making mistakes, not just what your mistakes are. Nearly every example of poor writing will fit under one or more of the six reasons below.

THE ROOT CAUSES OF POOR WRITING
The writer:
- didn't know the subject.
- didn't know the audience.
- didn't start early enough.
- needs a refresher course in grammar.
- was trying to impress someone.
- was hiding something, trying to deceive.

Find out if any of these six apply to you. Focus your attention on correcting that fundamental problem (or problems), and you've taken a giant step to being a better writer.

THE SALAMI SOLUTION

Did you ever try to eat a whole salami in one bite? Don't try to do a whole writing project in one big push.

Just like a salami, a writing project should be sliced into bite-size tasks, pieces you can do one at a time. The work is more appealing that way and you're not as likely to quit halfway through.

How you slice a job into bite-size pieces depends on the job. This example, useful for some long business documents, could be used or adapted for many writing jobs:

Slice the Writing Into Small Jobs

- **Learn.** Read, talk with informed people. (See list below for other ideas on how to get the information you need.)
- **Plan.** Just a four-point outline often clarifies your writing plan. (See examples of good and poor outlines below.)
- **Draft.** Draft a few pages at a time.
- **Revise.** Cross out every useless word and sentence you can find. Get comments from others who know your subject and your audience.
- **Type it.** Get a typed version that is as close to your intended final version as reasonable.
- **Proofread.** Don't proofread until you've finished arranging your thoughts on paper and deleting the unnecessary words and sentences. If you correct spelling and punctuation before you've settled on what you want to say, you're just polishing air.

Some Other Ideas About Where You Can Get Information on Your Subject

- Persons in your organization, but perhaps in a different department, who have written on the same subject.
- Persons in your organization who deal with or know someone outside who is an expert on the subject.
- Reports on file written by your predecessor or your supervisor.
- The public library. If your question is a brief one, you may get the information you need simply by calling the reference desk.
- Sales materials, catalogs, owners' manuals, repair guides and annual reports prepared by your competitors, by your suppliers or by organizations in a business related to yours.
- Dictionaries, encyclopedias and almanacs.
- Government publications.
- Book stores.
- The reporting and editing staff of journals and magazines published for your industry.

Examples of Good and Poor Brief Outlines

A Good Brief Outline

1. "Review how number of direct accounts grew from 200 to 2,000 in four years."
2. "Number of new products introduced in that period. Maybe describe complexity of a couple."
3. "Number of employees in home office Sales Department grew by about 50 percent in those four years. (Check with Sales Director.)"
4. "Tell of increases in customer complaints in past two years, costs of taking back wrong merchandise (ask Accounting). Compare to expected sales increase if four new phone salespeople were added (ask Personnel, Sales)."

A Poor Brief Outline

1. "Introduction." (This word serves no purpose for you.)
2. "Nature of the sales problem." (So broad a phrase that it is of only a little help to you.)
3. "Emphasize lack of dollar sense." (Too broad to be of help in planning what you will say.)
4. "Make recommendations." (You will make your recommendations with or without this in your outline. Serves no planning purpose.)

BETTER MEMOS AND LETTERS

Four Things to Ask Yourself Before Writing a Memo or Letter

1. **"Do I know the subject?"** Do you know what you are talking about well enough to write about it?
2. **"Do I know the audience?"** You write one way for your immediate supervisor, another way for the levels of management above her or him. For example, the higher levels of management may need some background information your supervisor already has. If you are writing for people outside your department, they may need certain details already known in your area.
3. **"Just what am I trying to accomplish with this memo or letter?"** A lot of memos and letters are written to get someone to do something—but they never state the request. The writers seem to think the readers will guess at what is to be done. You are not being impolite, just direct, when you say *what* you would like done, *who* should do it and *when* it should be done.

YOUR LETTERS OR MEMOS SHOULD DO ONE OR MORE OF THESE THINGS

- Inform.
- Request.
- Record information for the file.
- Direct.

---

4. **"Is this memo (or letter) necessary?"** Maybe you don't have to write so many memos and letters. Maybe some of yours have simply added to the paper avalanche we are all trying to dig out from under. The worst memos are the unnecessary memos. The worst letters are the ones that should have been phone calls.

A Pattern to Keep In Mind When Writing a Memo or Letter

FIRST PART: **Information about why you are writing**

("I am writing to suggest a way to make invoice inspections more efficient.")

SECOND PART: **Information about the subject**

("Inspections are often done during peak billing periods. This slows up billing and the inspection of invoices, and creates more possibilities for error.")

THIRD PART: **Information that supports your statements**

("According to this year's plan, we'll have nine occasions when our people are supposed to inspect invoices and bill on the same day.")

FOURTH PART: **Remedies, solutions, suggestions, ideas, plans, actions already taken**

("Please let me know if the revised schedule shown below meets your approval. May I have your response by November 12?")

FIFTH PART: **Copies of supporting or helpful material; photocopies of documents the reader will probably need or want**

("Please see attached copies of this year's plan and the previous two years' records.")

Some readers want such details, others don't. Satisfy both types of readers by making the supporting details available separately.

Use This Checklist When Going Over Your Memos and Letters

1. Are the main ideas placed early in the piece?
2. Are the later parts arranged logically?
3. Are there headings to aid the reader?
4. Are details relegated to attachments?
5. Is the needed action expressed clearly?

What Is a Logical Arrangement of Points in Memos and Letters?

There are several choices of logical order. Use one of these or devise your own as appropriate to meet the needs of the job.
• **Chronological:** Points arranged in the order they happened or should happen.
• **Order of importance:** From the most important to the least important.
• **Cause and effect:** State what was done and what resulted.
• **From the general to the specific (usually better than from the specific to the general):** Start with broad statements—"We need a new phone system"—and give the advantages or reasons after that.
• **Pros and cons:** Give the reasons for and against something. This is often best when a decision isn't yours to make and you want your supervisor to be able to weigh all the facts before making the decision.

Six Myths About the People Who Read Memos and Letters

It is a myth that people who read your memos and letters are...

...the people you address them to. The recipient may be your boss, but the audience may include your boss's boss, auditors, government regulatory agencies, secretaries and people who like to peck at other people's mail.
...specialists in your field. Give the special information your

readers need in order to understand your memo or letter. Your specialized language may be Greek to them or they may lack background information on your project.

...involved in daily discussions on the subject. Tell your reader just what you are talking about. Don't assume that your readers are tuned in to the same matters you are or that they have high priorities on the same projects you do.

...familiar with your responsibilities. Even your co-workers might not know just what your responsibilities are. Consider giving your readers some idea of what your part is in the subject at hand.

...awaiting your report. Many recipients have a stack of other memos, letters, an industry journal and a newsletter or two in their in-box. Give your reader a reason to get to yours first.

...able to read them as soon as they get them. If you need immediate action, maybe you should call instead of write. You can follow up with a memo or letter later if necessary.

Making Memos Talk

The personal tone of a memo can make even the driest subject interesting. To get that personal tone, write so that you seem to be talking to the reader. Here's how:

Use personal pronouns. "**I** am writing to ask **you** for the reports schedule." How much better that is than, "The reports schedule should be provided."

Drop the stiff, formal phrases. Most business people prefer the casual and direct style to the style our grandfathers used.

• **Old Style:** "Upon receipt of the order, our engineering department will be instructed to begin assembly."

• **Casual and direct:** "I'll have our engineers assemble your unit when the order arrives."

Use contractions where they sound right as you read aloud. You'll put a little personal quality, a human touch, in your writing if you use a contraction here and there. Read your material to yourself. "I *haven't* gotten your letter (yes, 'gotten' is a real word)" sounds friendlier than, "I *have not* received your letter."

Put yourself in the reader's place. Imagine you are the person the memo is addressed to. How does that person talk and think? What usually persuades him or her—brief arguments or long ones with many details included? Does the person use a large and diverse vocabulary or a simplified one?

BETTER REPORTS

Much of what appears in the Better Memos and Letters chapter applies to writing better reports. For example, see the questions you should ask yourself before writing, myths about readers and logical arrangements of points.

Features That Should Be in Most Reports

Some reports are written in memo form, some are written as letters, and some as formal reports. Here are the key elements that should be in most reports.

Title on the cover page.

Your name and the date on the cover page, perhaps with your signature, phone number and address.

The table of contents on the next page if the body of the report is three pages or longer.

The summary. Often, this can be on the cover page. If you don't put it there, put it right after the table of contents on a page by itself or at the top of the first page of text. This is probably the most important part of your report. Make it good.

The introduction, or background. This section tells why the report is necessary and which questions, needs or difficulties led to it being written. It should focus the reader's attention on what follows.

The body of the report. This consists, usually, of the methods you followed, the facts you uncovered (results or findings) and your comments on those facts. Select a limited number of points and stick to them.

The conclusion, usually with your recommendations. Sometimes writers confuse conclusions with a summary. Conclusions are what your thinking led you to when you used the facts in the report.

The appendix or appendices, if necessary.

The Importance of the Summary

Some years ago, Westinghouse Electric Corporation asked business people which parts of a report they read. Here are the results:
- 100 percent read the summary.
- 65 percent read the introduction.
- 22 percent read the body.
- 55 percent read the conclusions.
- 22 percent read the appendices.

Obviously, you have to say what you have to say in the summary if you want to get your message across. How do you write a good summary?

Typically, the first one or two sentences of a summary should give the *background*, answering questions of *who, when* and *why*. For example: "New Stone Corporation launched a campaign in July 1989 to increase annual sales by 15 percent."

The next few sentences usually answer *how* and *what*. For example: "Field sales representatives trained for one week before the campaign with the new descriptive literature, the designers' explanations and updated market research results. Their goals were: (1) making more calls on volume buyers, (2) answering technology questions on the spot rather than by phone days later, (3) getting a yes or clearly understood objectives at the end of the call."

The next sentences focus on *outcome*, and usually answer questions of *how* or *how much* and *what*. For example: "At the end of five weeks, calls on volume buyers are up 34 percent, sales are up 17 percent, and technical inquiries to the home office are down 80 percent."

The last sentence in a summary should answer the question: "What do you, the report writer, think of this?" Tell the reader your *conclusions* based on the facts. For example, is the campaign a worthwhile use of company resources? Should it be changed? Extended? Shortened? Repeated? You are presumably more familiar with the facts than anyone else. Give others the benefit of your thinking about the facts. For example: "The campaign is a success, but fine-tuning it may produce more sales increases."

Commonly Asked Questions About Summaries

The three questions asked most often about summaries are: (1) Should things like cost justification go in a summary? (2) How long should a summary be? (3) Can tables or graphs be used in a summary?

Important points such as cost justification definitely belong in the summary. If you know that one of the first things readers would ask about is cost justification, then put the cost justification in the summary.

The length of a summary varies with the length of a report. Short reports require shorter summaries. Most summaries run 100—300 words. And yes, you can use tables and graphs in a summary. Anything that puts the main points across quickly can be used.

One means of condensing a summary is to write it in a "bulleted" format as shown below.

Example of a bulleted summary:

Report Summary

- Objective: 15 percent sales increase. Tactics: One-week sales training, emphasis on technology.
- Sales reps' goals: More calls on volume buyers, more technology questions answered on the spot, yes response or clearly stated objection from customer.
- After five weeks: Calls on volume buyers up 34 percent, sales up 17 percent, technology questions to home office down 80 percent.
- Conclusions: Campaign should be continued two more months, then we should fine-tune training based on sales representatives' feedback to see if further sales increases are possible.

Report Format and Content: The Package and the Merchandise

One of the best ways to get started writing a report is to look at a report format. It starts you thinking about what you want in your report and where it should go. But remember that no one format is right for every report. Customize your report format to suit the content. As famed architect Frank Lloyd Wright put it, "Form follows function."

Don't Reinvent the Report

Your department or company may already have a standard report format. Checking with some of the experienced employees may save you a lot of time and work.

If the report you're writing is the first one you will have done for your boss, ask her or him if there are any that should be used as a guide. Also, check with co-workers who have recently filed reports and find out what feedback they got.

Know Why You're Writing the Report

Are you writing the report just to meet company policy? That's a poor reason, and you'll probably write a poor report. Are you writing it to get a promotion or raise? Those may be valid secondary reasons, but they aren't good primary reasons. A report should be written to *help someone make decisions*. If your report isn't designed to do that, it won't be of much use to you or anyone else.

Five Questions to Ask Before Writing a Report

1. **For whom is this report being written?** Your boss? Members of other departments? Persons outside the organization? You need to know so you can give whatever background or details are appropriate.

2. **What is the purpose of the report?** Should it persuade? (See "How to Persuade Instead of Just Inform.") Is it supposed to justify an expense? Should it simply present the facts? Are legal issues involved?

3. **When is the rough draft due?** When someone says the report has to be done by a particular date, they may mean only a draft for review or they may mean the final version. Clarify that point.

4. **Who is going to review it before it goes out?** Knowing who the reviewers are will help you write and plan your schedule. If only two persons have to check it, that's one thing. If a half dozen are going to see it, you might want to arrange a "meeting of the minds" so you can all go over the draft together. Otherwise, you might spend days trying to get all changes agreed on.

5. **When is the final version due?** Report writers sometimes don't want to bring up the subject of a due date because they don't want to hear, "It's due tomorrow." But if you don't bring the subject up, you don't get a chance to negotiate a due date. You run the risk that someone will walk into your office and say, "I thought you knew it was due today."

The "So What?" Test

When you have finished a draft of your report, read each paragraph and ask, "So what?" in the same way a new reader might. If the answer isn't in that same paragraph or the ones immediately following, you're off the track. Keep asking "So what?" as you go through the report. Test not only each paragraph, but each table, graph, chart and illustration. You might be surprised at how much you can leave out.

A Suggested Outline
for Trip Reports

If your office doesn't have a standard format for trip reports, use this one or adapt it.

- *Title* (or if your trip report is on memo paper, *Subject*); your name; date of the report; any other needed identification such as your department or section name.

- *Table of contents*, if the trip report is more than three pages long.
- *Summary*.
- The *purpose* of the trip.
- *Activities*.
- *Accomplishments*.
- *Recommendations*.
- *Attachments*.

Titles of trip reports, like other report titles, should convey a message such as, "Increase in Sampling Did Not Improve Quality Control."

A **table of contents** and a **summary** aren't necessary if your report is one or two pages long, but use them when your report will cover three or more pages.

The **purpose** of your trip. In giving this information, tell what project you were working on and how the trip was supposed to further that work. Did you go to study quality control techniques? To learn about new technology? To buy equipment? To meet people important in your work? To check on competitors' activities?

In the purpose section, give the dates of your trip and the places visited. If those facts don't fit here, be sure they are mentioned somewhere early in the report, such as in a subheading under the title or in the next section under Activities.

Activities (The methods or procedures you followed). When the reader knows how you did your work, he or she has a better idea of how reliable the information is. For example, what you learn in casual conversation has one type of reliability, what you hear in a speech at a meeting has another, and what you learn from a published report has another.

What you accomplished will usually be the most important part of the trip report. It doesn't have to be lengthy, but it does deserve a major part of your writing time. Take care with it.

Some examples of accomplishments are:
- Gained knowledge of how to do your job better.
- Contracts were signed.
- Sales presentations were made.
- New clients or potential customers were met.
- Prospective employees were scouted.
- Information on what the competition is doing was gathered, or new technology was learned.

Recommendations. This is where you show how the organization is going to benefit from your trip. Should different tactics be used to meet the competition? Should customers be handled differently? How can the knowledge that you brought back be put to use? What should be purchased? From whom, and at what price? Do you recommend that you or someone else take the same or a similar trip soon?

Attachments. It's always a good idea to bring back pamphlets, brochures and booklets from a trip because they will help you write the trip report. But don't make the mistake of simply attaching them to your report and telling readers, "Read the attached material to find out what's new." You have an obligation to direct readers' attention in the report to what is important and how it should be interrupted. If all you did was bring back printed material, your boss could just use the mail the next time.

BETTER PARAGRAPHS

Most writers make significant improvements in their paragraphing by giving attention to just two things: *topic sentences* and *relevance*.

The topic sentence generally belongs at the beginning of the paragraph in business writing. It's the sentence that tells the reader the main point of the paragraph. You can increase the *dramatic* effect of your paragraph if you save the topic sentence till the end, but you may exasperate your reader if you do. Remember, you're writing a business document, not a suspense novel.

Relevance. If you make each sentence add to or explain what you say in your topic sentence, you have relevance. If you find that some of the sentences don't relate to the topic sentence, you've either wandered off your subject or you need to start a new paragraph.

Transition is a little overrated. Every paragraph doesn't have to end with something that leads to the next paragraph, nor does each new paragraph have to begin with something that refers to the previous paragraph. Transition isn't bad, it just isn't required every time you start a new paragraph.

When you want transition between paragraphs, one of these four methods should help you.

Transition Method 1: Use a word or words in the first sentence of a new paragraph that are in the last line of the previous paragraph. Here's an example:

> If medical students don't learn good manners while they are learning medicine, they will be at a great disadvantage in dealing with colleagues, staff and *patients*.

> I once asked a student to examine the abdomen of a *patient* lying in an outpatient cubicle. He dashed in where she lay, flung back the blanket, plumped his hand on her abdomen and

shouted, "Gosh, what a beauty" (he was referring to the patient's enlarged spleen and not to her personal appearance), and dashed out again.

—Adapted from *Richard Asher Talking Sense*, The Pitman Press, Bath, England, 1973.

Transition Method 2: Use a word at the beginning of a paragraph that makes sense only when read in relation to the previous paragraph. *First* is such a word, as in "*First*, decide if transition is really needed to keep your reader with you."

Other transition words and phrases to use at the beginning of a new paragraph are:

Meanwhile,	*Later,*
Of course,	*Lately,*
Nevertheless,	*In the future,*
Because of this,	*More specifically,*
For example,	*More important,*
	(Not, by the way, *More importantly*.)

Transition Method 3: Use a single sentence as a paragraph between the two paragraphs you want to link. Make it refer both to the one before and the one after. For example:

The reports showed that miles driven increased as price-per-gallon decreased. Some tire manufacturers therefore wanted to keep gas prices down, either through action by the government or by action of their own manufacturers' association.

Economists pointed out, however, that there isn't always a clear cause-and-effect relationship between gas prices and the miles we drive.

They showed, for example, that mileage went up when car prices were down, too, and when foreign travel costs rose. Five years before, gas prices fell 18 percent but mileage fell almost 12 percent because weather across the nation was unusually bad.

Transition Method 4: Use a side heading or a paragraph heading to announce what the next paragraph is about. In the heading used here, *Transition Method 4* is all the transition needed to move the reader's concentration from the third paragraph to this one.

BETTER SENTENCES

Sentences and Machines

*"A sentence should contain no unnecessary words,
a paragraph no unnecessary sentences, for the same
reason that a drawing should have no unnecessary
lines and a machine no unnecessary parts. This requires
not that the writer make all his sentences short, or
that he avoid all detail and treat his subjects only in
outline, but that every word tell."*

Strunk, W and White, EB: *The Elements of Style*, New York, MacMillan Co, 1959, p ix.

E.B. White, co-author of the above book and one of America's most respected writers and editors, said that his technique for writing consisted of "getting rid of the unnecessary words." When you've cut away the unnecessary words and thoughts, what you have left is the core, the nugget of your message. That's what your readers want.

Some Formulas to Help You Write Better Sentences. Take Your Pick— But Remember, Formulas Only Help

Formula 1: Look at any 150 words in your writing. Count the number of one-syllable words. Divide the number by 10 and subtrac the result from 20. The number you get is the number of years of school your readers need to read your writing easily.

For example, let's say you find:

- 60 one-syllable words out of 150 consecutive words.
- Divide 60 by 10. You get 6.
- Subtract 6 from 20. You get 14.
- 14 is the grade level your writing is appropriate for—high school plus two years of college.

The tougher the intellectual challenge to the reader, the simpler your writing should be. If the subject is hard to understand ("Brain Surgery Self-Taught in Your Kitchen"), write one or two levels below your audience's highest reading capability.

What level do you think *The New York Times, Forbes Magazine* and *The Wall Street Journal* are written for? Grades 8 through 12. Most of their readers probably *could* handle nuclear physics and 17th century poetry with one half of their brain tied behind their back, but the editors and writers know that the readers want their business information fast and uncomplicated. Your audiences usually want the same.

Formula 2: Look for prefixes such as "pre-," "anti-" and "multi-." Look for suffixes such as "-ability," "-tion" and "-ism." See how many you can take out and replace with simpler words without sacrificing meaning. *Example*: A lawyer writes that "the order was nondischargeable." The root word is "charge." We have to process two prefixes, "non-" and "dis-," to get to it. Then we have to process "-able" with the rest of the word. A few more words like that and you feel like you're wading through wet cement to get to the meaning in a sentence.

"The order couldn't be carried out" takes two more words, but the meaning comes across faster.

Formula 3: Write sentences that have an average of 15—22 words, and write none longer than 40 words. (This is adapted from a guideline some newspapers use.) Long sentences slow up comprehension because they contain many elements that have to be related to one another.

How to Choose the Best Words

Use Concrete Instead of Abstract Terms

Use concrete terms rather than abstract words when you have a choice. Concrete things are things we can touch, see, taste, smell or hear—we know them through one or more of our five senses. Abstract things are known to us only by mental processes.

Poetry is an **abstract** term, *poem* is a **concrete** term. *Safety* is an **abstract** term, *accident-free days* is a **concrete** term.

So often, the writing that doesn't get results is filled with abstract terms. Imagine two groups of managers: one group is told they will be rewarded for increases in safety, the other is told they will be rewarded for increases in the number of their workers who are accident-free. Which do you think will have a better grasp of the job? **Concrete terms are better in most business writing simply because most business writing is about things that are real or tangible.**

Use Specific Terms Instead of General Terms

Soon is general, on *July 31 of this year* is specific. *Increased production* is general, *a 15-percent increase* is specific.

Use Simple Terms Instead of Complex Terms

"He maneuvered the hydrogen hydroxide control valve to the open position." Some folks actually write like that. Why not, "He turned the water on"?

Five Cures for Sick Sentences

Sometimes you know your sentences just aren't right but you're not quite sure why. Here are five cures that often are the only medicine they need.

1. Get rid of the anemic introductory phrases. Examples of anemic introductory phrases are:
- "There is."
- "There are."
- "It appears."
- "I would hope that."

These phrases say virtually nothing and, because they are at the beginning of sentences or clauses, what comes after them is often lifeless.
Compare:

> **anemic:** *There is* a difficulty with the accounts receivable being received on time.
> **strong:** Customers aren't paying us promptly.

"I would hope that" is another weak introductory phrase. It is the grammatical equivalent of a whimper. It says that under some circumstance the writer would like something to happen. But we don't care about what he or she might hope for under some unspecified circumstance—we want information.

> **whimper:** *I would hope that* dividends will not be paid late.
> **direct:** Dividends must be paid on schedule.

2. Get rid of the unnecessary prepositions. Prepositions are words such as:

> on, up, beside, before, behind, between, against, for, off, despite, by, in, into, out, among, across, toward, without, under, onto.

Before we realize it, we fill a sentence with prepositions, making the meaning cloudy and the sentence structure awkward. Compare these two versions of a sentence, one with a lot of prepositions, the other with most of them taken out.

> Tests *of* the machinery *on* the day *before* it was put *into* operation brought *out* defects *in* two *of* the four functions which had been specified *by* our shop workers. (Eight prepositions, a total of 30 words.)

> Tests done the day *before* we used the machines showed defects *in* two *of* the four functions our shop workers had specified. (Three prepositions, only 22 words in all.)

3. Break long sentences into two sentences. This is one of the easiest ways to cure a sick sentence and it is one of the best things you can do to increase your reader's comprehension.

Look for sentences that have 25 words or more. Make two—or even three—sentences of them, particularly when you are writing about something technical or complicated.

Often, the sentences that should be made into two shorter sentences are the ones with semicolons in them. When you see one, ask yourself whether the meaning would come across better if you put a period in place of the semicolon and started a new sentence there. *Example:*

> If we make six departments out of the present four, we'll need more managers; quite likely, we'll make communication among departments more difficult, too.

Take the semicolon out and start a new sentence:

> If we make six departments out of the present four, we'll need more managers. We'll probably make communication among departments more difficult, too.

4. Don't back into your sentences. "Backing into" a sentence is starting to talk about the subject before you say what the subject is. *Example:*

> *Believing that significant savings can be made and that no additional time will be required for the same results*, I am proposing the changes listed in this report.

The writer started with that long, backing-in phrase and kept us waiting till the end to find out what he or she was talking about. Readers often don't bother to finish that kind of sentence. Use some introductory phrases, but keep them short and don't use them too frequently.

5. Delete every unnecessary word. "He won a prize" says the same thing as "He won a *free* prize." "Experience" is the same as "*previous* experience." What about "*advance* reservations"—are there any other kind?

Do you need to say, "We'll plan for the future"? "We'll plan" conveys the message, but less pompously.

You can cut the number of your words by a significant amount by looking for ones like these. The benefit to you is that you sharpen your message. The benefit to your readers is they don't have to slog through so many words to get the message.

DON'T WRITE:	DO WRITE:
Prior to . . . . *Before*
Upon that date . . . . *On that date,* or *then*
At that point in time . . . . *Then*
At this point in time . . . . *Now*
Past experience . . . . *Experience*
10 a.m. in the morning . . . . *10 a.m.*
They each shared a common goal . . . . . . *They had the same goal*
Potential hazard . . . . *Hazard*
Possible danger . . . . *Danger*

Twelve of the Most Commonly Confused Word Pairs

Knowing how to use these words will sharpen the messages you put across to your readers.

Fewer, less. In general, use *fewer* for individual items, *less* for bulk or quantity.

> Right: I had less than $100 when I returned from vacation. (an amount)
>
> Right: I had fewer than 100 $1 bills in my wallet. (individual items)
>
> Wrong: This year's convention had more speakers and less participants. (Participants refers to individuals.)
>
> Wrong: He was fewer than 80 years old. (Years refers to a period of time, not individual years.)

Among, between. Use *among* when more than two things are involved, *between* when only two are involved. It is incorrect to say, "The agreement between the three directors." You should say, "The agreement among the three directors."

Anxious, eager. Anxious means worried or uneasy. Eager means enthusiastic. Taxpayers are anxious to see how the new tax laws will work. Tax lawyers are eager to get the new business they will bring.

Remember, eager = enthusiastic.

Imply, infer. Imply is what people do when they hint at something or express something indirectly. Put another way, when they imply, they cause an idea to fly to the audience.

Infer is what we in the audience do when we form a conclusion from what the speaker or writer says. We infer, but we can't be sure. Presume is a synonym for infer. "The boss implied that costs would go down; we inferred that some salaries would be cut."

Remember: When you imply, you make an idea fly. When you infer, you can't be sure.

Fortuitous, fortunate. Fortuitous means happening by chance, and it can refer to *good* luck or *bad* luck. About half the time, fortuitous events are "do-it-to-us" events. You can be late because of a fortuitous flat tire; you are fortunate if your spare isn't flat, too.

Remember: Fortuitous events may be "do-it-to-us" events.

Gratuitous, gracious. Gratuitous simply means uncalled for, not earned, out of place.

Remember it this way: Most *gratuitous* things *grate* on our nerves.

Affect, effect. Each of these words can be used as a noun and as a verb. Use these memory aids to keep the usage straight.

Affect as a *noun* refers to a person's mood or feelings. For example, psychiatrists refer to the listless, uninvolved mood of some mentally ill patients as a flat affect. (Associate the *a* in affect with the *a* in flat.)

Affect as a *verb* refers to causing an influence on something. Nothing affects the flat affect of some patients.

Now move on in the alphabet from *a* to *e*. Effect as a noun refers to something that follows a cause or a force. "A two-by-four has no effect in making them heed what is said." (Use the *e*'s to help you remember.)

Effect as a *verb* means to bring something into being. "To effect a change (bring it into being), you need more than energy." (Again, the sentence that helps you remember has several *e*'s.)

Memorize these sentences and you've got it made. To help you remember, notice there are *a*'s and *e*'s in the key words:

Nothing *affects* the flat *affect* of some patients. A two-by-four has no *effect* on making them heed. To *effect* a change, you need more than energy.

Verbal, spoken. Verbal has been misused for so long that it's hard to get even some linguists to use it correctly. But there is a distinction between verbal and spoken that is worth your while. Verbal simply means expressed by word, either spoken or written. If someone says, "A verbal agreement will be sufficient," he or she hasn't ruled out a written agreement.

When you think you want to say verbal, you probably mean spoken.

Initials, acronym. NBC is a set of initials or an initialism, not an acronym. MOMA is an acronym, a set of initials for the Museum of Modern Art, that can be spoken as a word. Radar is another acronym. It was spelled with all capital letters for several years—RADAR—because it stands for radio detection and ranging. Remember, acronyms can be spoken as words ("MOMA"), initials cannot.

Bring, take. Standing in your office, you would not be grammatically correct to say to a co-worker, "Bring this to Ed on the first floor on your way out, will you?"

The word you want in that sentence is *take*. Use take when the action is away from the place from which the action is regarded. Use bring when the action is toward the place from which the action is regarded.

Think of yourself as the center of action, then remember the two most familiar phrases in which those terms are used—"bring to" and "take away."

Persuade, convince. You persuade *to*, you convince *that*. It is proper to say, "He persuaded me to look at the report," not "He convinced me to look at the report." If you want to use the word convinced in the sentence, you say, "He *convinced* me that I should look at the report."

Remember, persuade *to*, convince *that*.

Accept, except. These are prize winners when they get mixed up. A restaurant owner did it once with this sign at his cash register: "We except only MasterCard and Visa." Either he had used the wrong word or he had gone to some bother to prohibit the use of two popular credit cards at his place.

Accept: receive willingly. Except: leave out, reject.

Some People Are Afraid of *Me*, But They Like *I* and *Myself*

Quite a few people are afraid of *me*. Nearly everybody likes *I* and *myself*, but for some reason they are afraid of *me*.

For example, instead of saying, "Thanks for inviting my wife and me," they say, "Thanks for inviting my wife and I," or "my wife and myself." If I hadn't invited their wives, would they say, "Thanks for inviting I"? Or "Thanks for inviting myself"?

The way to avoid mistakes like this is to take the other person or persons out of the sentence. For example:

"Thanks for inviting my wife and I."

becomes

"Thanks for inviting I? me?" The correct choice—*me*—is obvious to us when the other person is taken out of the sentence.

"The plan prepared by Bert and (I?, me?) was approved."

becomes

"The plan prepared by I? me? was approved." The correct choice—*me*—is again obvious.

GRAMMAR HOTLINES— ALMOST AS GOOD AS BEING SMART

Numbers You Can Call for Answers to Questions on Grammar, Spelling, Capitalization, Punctuation

Some good-hearted souls at colleges and universities around the country will listen to our questions over the phone and try to figure out what we should be doing. The services operate with student and faculty volunteers during usual business hours. When you call, allow for differences in time zones; you pay the long-distance cost.

You'll get the best help when you can clearly describe what you're trying to do. Be ready to explain the context and the exact writing problem.

Other possible sources of help: the English department at a nearby university or college, the reference desk at your public library.

A list of grammar hotlines begins below.

ALABAMA
Auburn University, Auburn, 36830
Monday through Thursday, 9 a.m. to noon and 1 p.m. to 4 p.m.
Friday, 9 a.m. to noon; reduced hours during summer
(205) 826-5749—Writing Center Hotline

ARKANSAS
University of Arkansas at Little Rock, Little Rock, 72204
Monday through Friday, 8 a.m. to noon
(501) 569-3162—The Writer's Hotline

CALIFORNIA
Moorpark College, Moorpark, 93021
Monday through Friday, 8 a.m. to noon, September through June
(805) 529-2321—National Grammar Hotline

COLORADO
University of Southern Colorado, Pueblo, 81001
Monday through Friday, 9:30 a.m. to 3:30 p.m.; reduced hours
May 15 to August 25
(303) 549-2787—USC Grammar Hotline

FLORIDA
University School of Nova University, Ft. Lauderdale, 33314
Monday through Thursday, 8 a.m. to 4 p.m.; Friday, 8 a.m.
to 2 p.m.
(303) 475-7697—Grammar Hotline

University of West Florida, Pensacola, 32514
Monday through Thursday, 9 a.m. to 5 p.m.; occasional evening
hours; Friday and summer hours vary
(904) 474-2129—Writing Lab and Grammar Hotline

GEORGIA
Georgia State University, Atlanta, 30303
Monday through Thursday, 8:30 a.m. to 5 p.m.; Friday, 8:30 a.m. to
3 p.m.; evening hours vary
(404) 658-2906—Writing Center

ILLINOIS
Eastern Illinois University, Charleston, 61920
Monday through Friday, 10 a.m. to 3 p.m.; summer hours vary
(217) 581-5929—Grammar Hotline

Illinois State University, Normal, 61761
Monday through Friday, 8 a.m. to 4:30 p.m.
(304) 438-2345—Grammar Hotline

Triton College, River Grove, 60171
Monday through Thursday, 8:30 a.m. to 9 p.m.; Friday, 8:30 a.m. to
4 p.m.; Saturday, 10 a.m. to 1 p.m.
(312) 456-0300, ext. 254—Grammarphone

INDIANA
Indiana University—Purdue University at Indianapolis,
Indianapolis, 46202
Monday through Thursday, 9 a.m. to 4 p.m.
(317) 274-3000—IUPUI Writing Hotline

Ball State University, Muncie, 47306
Monday through Thursday, 8 a.m. to 8 p.m.; Friday, 8 a.m. to
5 p.m., September through May
(317) 285-8387—Grammar Crisis Line

Purdue University, West Lafayette, 47907
Monday through Friday, 9:30 a.m. to 4 p.m., when a writing
instructor is available, during spring, summer and fall semesters;
closed during May and August
(317) 494-3723—Grammar Hotline

KANSAS (also see Missouri)
Emporia State University, Emporia, 66801
Monday through Thursday, noon to 5 p.m.; Thursday night, 7 p.m.
to 9 p.m.; summer hours vary
(316) 343-1200—Writer's Hotline

Johnson County Community College, Overland Park
(913) 469-8500, ext. 3439

LOUISIANA
University of Southwestern Louisiana, Lafayette, 70504
Monday through Thursday, 8 a.m. to 4 p.m.; Friday, 8 a.m. to
1 p.m.
(318) 231-5224—Grammar Hotline

MARYLAND
University of Maryland—Baltimore County, Baltimore, 21228
Monday through Friday, 10 a.m. to noon, September through May
(301) 455-2585—Writer's Hotline

Frostburg State College, Frostburg, 21532
Monday through Friday, 10 a.m. to noon (accepts long-distance
calls—funded by Maryland Committee for the Humanities,
Frostburg State College Foundation, C & P Telephone Company)
(301) 689-4327

MASSACHUSETTS
North Shore Community College, Lynn, 01915
Monday through Friday, 8:30 a.m. to 4 p.m.
(617) 593-7284—Grammar Hotline

Northeastern University, Boston, 02115
Monday through Friday, 8:30 a.m. to 4:30 p.m.
(617) 437-2512—Grammar Hotline

MICHIGAN
C.S. Mott Community College, Flint, 48503
Monday through Thursday, 8:30 a.m. to 3:30 p.m.; Friday, 8:30
a.m. to 12:30 p.m.; Tuesday and Wednesday evenings, 5:30 p.m. to
8:30 p.m.; summer hours vary
(313) 762-0229—Grammar Hotline

Western Michigan University, Kalamazoo, 49008-3899
Monday through Friday, 9 a.m. to 4 p.m.; summer hours vary
(616) 383-8122—Writer's Hotline

MISSOURI
Missouri Souther State College, Joplin, 64801
Monday through Friday, 9 a.m. to 2 p.m.
(417) 624-0171—Grammar Hotline

University of Missouri at Kansas City, Kansas City, 64110-2499
Monday through Friday, 9 a.m. to 4 p.m., September through May;
summer hours vary
(816) 276-2244—Writer's Hotline

NEW YORK
York College of the City University of New York, Jamaica, 11451
Monday through Friday, 1 p.m. to 4 p.m.
(718) 739-7483—Rewrite

NORTH CAROLINA
Methodist College, Fayetteville, 28301
Monday through Friday, 8 a.m. to 5 p.m.
(919) 488-7110—Grammar Hotline

OKLAHOMA
Virginia Lee Underwood, Chickasha, 73018
Monday through Friday, 9 a.m. to 5 p.m.; Saturday, 9 a.m. to noon
Mrs. Underwood, retired teacher and editor, offers this service
through her home telephone. She is willing to return long-distance
calls collect.
(405) 224-8622

OHIO
Raymond Walters College, Cincinnati, 45236
Tapes requests—returns calls (long-distance calls returned collect)
(513) 745-4312—Dial-A-Grammar

University of Cincinnati, Cincinnati, 45221
Monday through Friday, 9 a.m. to 10 a.m. and noon to 2 p.m.
(513) 475-2493—Writer's Remedies

Cincinnati Technical College, Cincinnati, 45223
Monday through Thursday, 8 a.m. to 8 p.m.; Friday, 8 a.m. to
4 p.m.; Saturday, 9 a.m. to 1 p.m.
(513) 559-1520, ext. 202 or 133—Writing Center Hotline

Ohio Wesleyan University, Delaware, 43015
Monday through Friday, 9 a.m. to noon and 1 p.m. to 4 p.m.,
September through May
(614) 369-4431, ext. 301—Writing Resource Center

PENNSYLVANIA
Cedar Crest College, Allentown, 18104
Monday through Friday, 10 a.m. to 3 p.m., September through May
(215) 437-4471—Academic Support Center, Writing Center Hotline

Robert S. Burger, Glen Mills, 19342
Monday through Friday, 8 a.m. to 5 p.m.
Mr. Burger, formerly a teacher of writing and journalism at several
colleges, offers this service through his office, which conducts
courses in effective writing.
(215) 399-1130—Burger Associates

Lincoln University, Lincoln University, 19352
Monday through Friday, 9 a.m. to 5 p.m., September through May;
summer hours vary
(215) 932-8300, ext. 460—Grammar Hotline

SOUTH CAROLINA
The Citadel Writing Center, Charleston, 29409
Monday through Friday, 8 a.m. to 4 p.m.; Sunday through
Thursday, 6 p.m. to 10 p.m.
(803)792-3194—Grammar Hotline

University of South Carolina, Columbia, 29208
Monday through Thursday, 8:30 a.m. to 5 p.m.; Friday, 8:30 a.m. to
1 p.m.
(803) 777-7020—Writer's Hotline

TEXAS
University of Houston Downtown, Houston, 77002
Monday through Thursday, 9 a.m. to 4 p.m.; Friday, 9 a.m. to
1 p.m.; summer hours, Monday through Thursday, 10:30 a.m. to
4 p.m.

San Antonio College, San Antonio, 78284
Monday through Thursday, 8 a.m. to 9:45 p.m.; Friday, 8 a.m. to
4 p.m.
(512) 733-2503—Learning Line

WISCONSIN
Northeast Wisconsin Technical Institute, Green Bay, 54307-9042
Monday through Thursday, 8:30 a.m. to 8 p.m.; Friday, 8 a.m. to
4 p.m.
(414) 498-5427—Grammar Hotline

University of Wisconsin—Platteville, Platteville, 53818
Monday through Thursday, 9 a.m. to 4 p.m.; Friday, 9 a.m. to
1 p.m.
(608) 342-1615—Grammar Hotline

VIRGINIA
Tidewater Community College Writing Center, Virginia Beach,
23456
Monday through Friday, 10 a.m. to noon; afternoon hours vary;
reduced hours during summer
(804) 427-7170—Grammar Hotline

COMMON PUNCTUATION PROBLEMS AND SOLUTIONS

Plurals

Usually, add -s or -es.

pen	pens
church	churches
Rogers	Rogerses
	("Rogerss" would look weirder.)
tomato	tomatoes
potato	potatoes
radio	radios

Sometimes, change the word or use the same word.

man	men
woman	women
fish	fish
	(Or *fishes*, if you're a poet.)

Apostrophes don't add anything but the possibility of confusion to some plurals. *BVDs* is just as clearly plural as *BVD's*; the only difference is that a reader might think something belonged to the BVD's. Other plurals that don't need the apostrophe:

"There aren't two TWAs, you know. Only one."

"She'll be vice president by the end of the 1980s."

"There are nine PhDs here."

"The doctor recorded six EKGs."

The **rare** exception—to prevent misreading:
"Some of the do's and don'ts."
(It's better than "the dos and don'ts," less likely to be misread.)
"She got two A's on her research project."
(So it won't sound like "two As on her research project.")
"How many o's are there in this sentence?"
"Did the Oakland A's win?"

Forming Possessives

Singular nouns, add the apostrophe and s.
This hospital's units
Plural nouns ending in s, add only the apostrophe.
The two hospitals' units
Two years' experience
The Joneses' house
Singular nouns ending in s—add 's unless the next word begins in s.
Charles's job
Charles' sportscar
Singular nouns ending in z or x, you may add just the apostrophe, but most people add the apostrophe and s.
Fritz's riches
Xerox's machine
Karl Marx's theories
Plural nouns not ending in s, add apostrophe and s.
The people's right
Women's favorite
Men's wear
Children's lunches

Quotation Marks

Some people use quotation marks to emphasize words and they shouldn't. There's a story, perhaps true, that illustrates why it doesn't work.

A company president, according to the story, told his advertising copywriter to use more quote marks in the company ads, "to give the words a little more oomph, you know," he said. The copywriter listened but didn't say anything. He simply wrote something on a piece of paper and passed it across the desk to his boss. It read:

I understand you spent the weekend in Atlantic City with your "wife."

Quotation marks have only three uses:

- to show which words someone said.
- to enclose the title of a song, a story, a chapter in a book or some other short piece of work.
- to show you don't mean what you say—"I almost 'bought the farm' on that curve one night."

Quotation Marks and Question Marks

He asked, "Why do it?"
Did he say "Watch your beer"?
Did they play the "Star-Spangled Banner"?
Who asked "Where's your office?"

If the question mark refers to the words in the quote, it goes inside the quotation marks.

You never use *two* end punctuation marks (periods, exclamation marks, question marks) at the end of a sentence. Let the question mark, whether inside or outside the quotation marks, be the only end punctuation. It is *incorrect* to write:

He asked, "Why do it?".

Quotation Marks, Commas and Periods

They *always* go inside the end quotation marks.
"I hope you'll stay," they said.
"Sounds like a good offer. Sold."
He said "forty," "twenty," then "six" and "twelve."

You Don't Always Put Quote Marks at the End of a Paragraph

"Four of the eight units," she said, "will be opened by March 2, 1987. We're going to have to work hard and fast, there are going to be some problems we have to solve on the spot.

"Following the March 2 opening, we'll pace new construction more slowly. Then we'll have more time to plan for staffing them."

Because the speaker is continuing her remarks in the second paragraph, you **don't** show an end to her remarks in the first paragraph with quotation marks after *spot*. Rather, leave the quotation open and start the new paragraph with quote marks to show those are also her words. End the quote where she stops speaking, at the end of the second paragraph.

Commas Simplified

The things you need to keep in mind about commas are that they are used to help make meaning clear and make reading a little easier.*

If you're absolutely certain your meaning is clear without commas, leave them out. Someone put it into rhyme: *"If there's no doubt, leave them out."*

Here's a quick review of the most common comma usages. Use commas:

• **To separate items in a series:** "Your report will be reviewed by the vice presidents of Finance, Advertising and Quality Control." Notice that there is no comma before *and* in that sentence. That's the modern way. The rule used to be you **had** to put a comma after each item in a series, but today many grammarians say you need one before *and* only to prevent misreading, as in "There were flasks filled with various solutions: chloride, sodium, sugar, and potassium." Without the comma before *and*, the reader might well think one flask was filled with a solution of sugar and potassium.

---

*The idea that you put a comma in where you would pause if you were reading aloud is correct only up to a point. There are places where you would pause in reading where no comma is necessary, just as commas are necessary some places where you would not pause.

- **To set off long introductory phrases:** "Before the first run and before the tests were made on the output, we checked the fuel pressure." If you have a short introductory phrase, no comma is needed. "Before yesterday there was no test."
- **To prevent misreading:** "Before testing the boiler was dismantled" is wrong. The reader reads, "Before testing the boiler" as an introductory phrase before realizing the phrase was supposed to be just "Before testing." Write instead, " Before testing, the boiler was dismantled."
- **To set off appositives:** Appositives, in grammar, are words or phrases that repeat the nearby words. " This is *Rudy*, my *valet*."
- **To separate a string of adjectives:** "The report is a clear, concise, well-designed document." "I put a crisp, hard-earned buck in the machine." Note: No comma is needed to separate the adjectives when they are cumulative—that is, when their sequence can't be rearranged. "He wore a *dark silk* suit and a *20-karat gold* bracelet."
- **To set off quotations:** "Then she said, 'How about the budget?'"
- **To set off nonrestrictive clauses:** Nonrestrictive clauses are a lot like appositives. They repeat—and usually clarify—what was just said. " The two budgets, *which had been checked*, were approved." That says there were only two budgets. Notice the different meaning when you take the commas out. "The two budgets which had been checked were approved." That says of the many budgets, two were checked and approved. (Good grammarians point out that we should use *that* in place of *which* in that last example, but few English teachers cover that in class these days. Most feel the distinction is a lost cause.)
- **To set off the day of the month from the year:** September 26, 1987. Some grammarians say you need one after the year in the middle of a sentence, others say it isn't needed. "Meet me on September 26, 1988 in front of the courthouse." Follow the style acceptable to your organization and audience.

How to Use Hyphens

These little marks can be vital. If you ordered "100 foot lights" you'd get something quite different than if you ordered "100-foot lights."

"His fourth best selling novel" doesn't mean the same thing as "his fourth-best selling novel."

The surest way to find out whether a word should be hyphenated is to look it up in the dictionary.

The next best way is to keep these guidelines handy on your desk.

- **When two adjectives are being used as one modifier (describer) and they are in front of the word they modify, use a hyphen.** "That is the *best-known* product." "That product is *best known*."
- **When one of the modifying words is an adverb ending in -ly, leave the hyphen out.** "That's a beautifully made desk."
- **Use a hyphen after ex-, self- and all-.** "Ex-wife," "self-inflicted," "all-conference."
- **When you have a series of hyphenated modifiers, carry the hyphen over like this:** "Replace the second-, third-, fourth- and fifth-story windows."
- **Use the hyphen to prevent confusion.** "Re-sign" means something completely different from "resign."
- **Use a hyphen to prevent misreading or awkward spelling.** "Semi-invalid" instead of "semiinvalid."

HOW TO MAKE YOUR WORK EASIER TO READ

Headings help. In conversation, we use our hands, eyes and voices to signal an important point. In writing, headings help us do that.

Use lists. They often make details easier to grasp. The following paragraph and the list say the same thing. Which one is the busy reader more likely to prefer?

Version 1:

The treatment produced reductions in fever, decreases in swelling, increases in appetite, weight gain, sharper responses to stimuli and better coordination.

Version 2:

Treatment produced favorable changes in:

- temperature
- swelling
- appetite
- body weight
- responses to stimuli
- coordination

Use indented paragraphs. That's what our eyes are used to. From the first grade on, everything we've read—school books, newspapers, magazines, novels—has had indented paragraphs. Why then do we often find block paragraphs in business correspondence? Because early manual typewriters didn't have tabs for indented paragraphs, and today some of us are following the path laid down by typing teachers and textbooks years ago.

Our eyes and our minds are trained to recognize indented paragraphs as the beginnings of new chunks of information. The beginnings of block paragraphs are not noticeable when side headings are used, when new paragraphs begin at the top of a page, and when text resumes below a table or illustration on a page.

With modern typewriters and word processors, there isn't much reason to use block paragraphs. Give your readers what they are most comfortable with—indented paragraphs.

COPYRIGHT IS FREE AND SIMPLE

Y ou wouldn't believe that anything that's under the control of lawyers and government would be free and simple, but copyright is. All you have to do is claim copyright, like this: **Copyright © National Seminars, Inc., 1989**.

In fact, you have copyright even when you don't claim it. The interpretation of the law runs this way: from the time the creator of something picks up his or her pen, copyright is in force. (Yes, you can go to Washington and file a paper and pay a fee, but that's necessary only in unusual circumstances.)

You can put a copyright notice on anything you write—reports, ads, newsletters. The notice gives you protection under the law, thus discouraging pirates and copiers.

Want more information on copyright? Write to:

Copyright Office
Library of Congress
Washington, D.C. 20559

Ask for the free booklet, "Highlights of the New Copyright Law," circular R99.

PEOPLE LOVE TO BICKER ABOUT...

There are some matters in English that aren't worth bickering about.

Plural: data, **Singular:** data or datum?

politics	politic?
news	new?
agenda	agendum?

We don't say, "Those are interesting political news. I'll make a note on my agendum to read more about them. Politics are dirty businesses, aren't they?"

Recognize that some words are plural in form but singular in construction like: news, politics. Others have been made singular by our usage over the years, like agenda. Some can be singular or plural, depending on which side of the argument you want to take, like data. Try to agree on a style manual to be used in your office. Sometimes, just agreeing on which dictionary to use in the office is a big help. *Websters New World Dictionary, Third College Edition* and the *American Heritage Dictionary of the English Language* are popular ones. If you choose one of them, you'll find it fairly easy to get agreement on style around your office.

IF YOU COULD HAVE ONLY THREE BOOKS BESIDES THIS ONE...

Nearly everyone who writes will benefit from these three books. If you have room for only this book and three others on your desk, these are the ones to have.

To improve style and clarity, for good writing principles: *The Elements of Style*, third edition, by William Strunk, Jr., and E.B. White, MacMillan Publishing Co, Inc., New York, 91 pages. It was written by Professor Strunk in the early 1900s for his Cornell University students and updated by E.B. White, a former student, in 1958. It has gained in popularity over the years to the point where it is commonly referred to simply as "Strunk and White" or "the little book." It's lively and clear and one of the few books on writing that is enjoyable. You'll improve virtually every time you read—or reread—a page.

The best of the desk dictionaries: *The American Heritage Dictionary of the English Language*, edited by William Morris, Houghton Mifflin Company, Boston, 1550 pages. All dictionaries are not created equal. Some simply list the meanings and pronunciations that are *common*. Others, like this one, tell you what the *best* choices are. If you choose a dictionary that gives you the here-today-gone-tomorrow language of teeny-boppers and demagogues, you risk having more misunderstandings.

Good dictionaries like *The American Heritage Dictionary* tell you what is widely accepted among experts. This one has a panel of more than 150 members. The panel includes such eminent writers as Arthur Schlesinger, Jr., Paul Theroux, Neil Simon and Peter De Vries. From the world of journalism there are authorities such as

Bill Moyers, Russel Baker and Mary McGrory. From politics there are such respected speakers and writers as Daniel Moynihan, Eugene McCarthy and Stewart Udall. These people know language and can distinguish between trends and fads, and between almost-right words and the right word.

A book to help you with the tough grammar questions.
The Harbrace College Handbook, 10th edition, by John C. Hodges and Mary E. Whitten, Harcourt Brace Jovanovich, Publishers, San Diego, 553 pages. This is one of several good ones you'll find in any bookstore. Whichever grammar book you buy, get a recent edition. English, like everything else, changes over time. What we were taught as "the only right way" in school may now be only one of two or three correct choices.

THERE'S AN OLD SAYING...

This is a collection of old sayings about writing that have been around a long time. There's a nugget of help in all of them.

"**Hard writin' makes easy readin'.**" And writing done with little or no effort makes hard reading.

"**Hardly anybody likes to write, nearly everybody likes having written.**" If you find writing is difficult, you have company. Lots of it.

"**Writing is thinking captured on paper.**" If your thinking isn't clear, your writing won't be either.

"**If you know it, you can say it. If you can say it, you can write it.**" When you're having trouble writing something, just say what you're trying to write. A successful novelist I know picks out someone when he begins a book and "tells" the story, beginning to end, to him or her.

"**Starting to write a long piece without an outline is like taking off on a cross-country trip without a map.**"

"**I would have written a shorter report, but I didn't have the time.**" Long, rambling pieces are easy to write. Condensing your writing—getting all the unnecessary words and thoughts out—is what takes time. Allow for it in your scheduling.

And the final one, for your use when your critics can only tell you how they would have written something ("You should have done this, you should have done that, I would have done this" and on and on...): "**Where were you when the paper was blank?**"

Notes

Notes

Notes

Notes

Notes

Notes

Buy two, get one free!

Each of our handbook series (*LIFESTYLE, COMMUNICATION, PRODUCTIVITY* and *LEADERSHIP*) was designed to give you the most comprehensive collection of hands-on desktop references all related to a specific topic. Plus at the unbeatable offer of buy two, get one free, you can't find higher quality learning resources for less! **To order**, see the back of this page for the entire handbook selection.

1. Fill out and send the entire page by mail to:

In U.S.A.	**In Canada**
National Press Publications	**National Press Publications**
6901 West 63rd Street	10 Newgale Gate, Unit #4
P.O. Box 2949	Scarborough, Ontario M1X 1C5
Shawnee Mission, Kansas 66201-1349	

2. Or *FAX 1-913-432-0824*

3. Or call toll-free *1-800-258-7246* (in Kansas, 1-913-432-7757)

Fill out completely:

Name _____

Organization _____

Address_____

City _____

State/Province _____ Zip/Postal Code _____

Telephone ( )_____

Method of Payment

☐ Enclosed is my check or money order
☐ Please charge to:
    ☐MasterCard   ☐Visa   ☐American Express

Signature _____ Exp. date_____

Credit Card Number

To order multiple copies for co-workers and friends:	**U.S.**	**Can.**
20—50 copies.........................	$8.50	$10.95
Over 50 copies.........................	$7.50	$ 9.95

LEADERSHIP

Qty.	Item #	Title	U.S. Price	Canadian Price	Total Due
	410	The Supervisor's Handbook, Revised and Expanded	$12.95	$14.95	
	458	Positive Performance Management: *A Guide to "Win-Win" Reviews*	$12.95	$14.95	
	459	Techniques of Successful Delegation	$12.95	$14.95	
	463	Powerful Leadership Skills for Women	$12.95	$14.95	
	494	Team-Building	$12.95	$14.95	
	495	How to Manage Conflict	$12.95	$14.95	

COMMUNICATION

Qty.	Item #	Title	U.S. Price	Canadian Price	Total Due
	413	Dynamic Communication Skills for Women	$12.95	$14.95	
	414	The Write Stuff: *A Style Manual for Effective Business Writing*	$12.95	$14.95	
	442	Assertiveness: *Get What You Want Without Being Pushy*	$12.95	$14.95	
	460	Techniques to Improve Your Writing Skills	$12.95	$14.95	
	461	Powerful Presentation Skills	$12.95	$14.95	
	482	Techniques of Effective Telephone Communication	$12.95	$14.95	
	485	Personal Negotiating Skills	$12.95	$14.95	
	488	Customer Service: *The Key to Winning Lifetime Customers*	$12.95	$14.95	

PRODUCTIVITY

Qty.	Item #	Title	U.S. Price	Canadian Price	Total Due
	411	Getting Things Done: *An Achiever's Guide to Time Management*	$12.95	$14.95	
	468	Understanding the Bottom Line: *Finance for Non-Financial Managers*	$12.95	$14.95	
	483	Successful Sales Strategies: A Woman's Perspective	$12.95	$14.95	
	489	Doing Business Over the Phone: *Telemarketing for the '90s*	$12.95	$14.95	
	496	Motivation & Goal-Setting: *The Keys to Achieving Success*	$12.95	$14.95	

LIFESTYLE

Qty.	Item #	Title	U.S. Price	Canadian Price	Total Due
	484	The Stress Management Handbook	$12.95	$14.95	
	486	Parenting: *Ward and June Don't Live Here Anymore*	$12.95	$14.95	
	487	How to Get the Job You Want	$12.95	$14.95	

Subtotal	
Special 3-book offer (U.S. $25.90; Can. $29.90)	
Kansas residents add 5.5% sales tax	
Shipping and handling ($1 one item/.50 each add. item)	
TOTAL	

Thank you for your Order!